BANDIT LETTERS

New Issues Poetry & Prose

Editor	Herbert Scott
Associate Editor	David Dodd Lee
Advisory Editors	Nancy Eimers, Mark Halliday, William Olsen, J. Allyn Rosser
Assistants to the Editor	Rebecca Beech, Marianne E. Swierenga
Assistant Editors	Erik Lesniewski, Carrie McGath, Lydia Melvin, Adela Najarro, Margaret von Steinen
Copy Editor	Dianna Allen
Editorial Assistants	Derek Pollard, Bethany Salgat
Business Manager	Michele McLaughlin
Fiscal Officer	Marilyn Rowe

New Issues Poetry & Prose
The College of Arts and Sciences
Western Michigan University
Kalamazoo, MI 49008

An Inland Seas Poetry Book

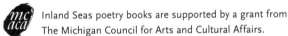 Inland Seas poetry books are supported by a grant from The Michigan Council for Arts and Cultural Affairs.

First Edition, 2001
ISBN: 1-930974-08-6 (paperbound)

Library of Congress Cataloging-in-Publication Data:
Messer, Sarah
Bandit Letters/Sarah Messer
Library of Congress Catalog Card Number: 2001131154

Art Direction:	Tricia Hennessy
Design:	Sarah Williams
Production:	Paul Sizer
	The Design Center, Department of Art
	College of Fine Arts
	Western Michigan University
Printing:	Courier Corporation

10-23-01

Michael McE~

Great to meet you. And I can't
wait to read your book filled
with smoke, static, & mufflers.

Here's to many more swap-sessions

Jay + luck to you +
yours

BANDIT LETTERS

SARAH MESSER

New Issues

WESTERN MICHIGAN UNIVERSITY

Contents

Acknowledgements

The author wishes to acknowledge the editors of the following journals in which some of the poems in this collection (often under different titles) first appeared:

Boulevard: "Song"

Cream City Review: "After wild fire"

The Journal: "With this change to indoor lighting"

Kenyon Review: "Some women marry houses"

Paris Review: "Gossip," "Hotel suicide," "In the market," "Rendered dog"

Pierogi Press: "I am the real Jesse James," "Rumor"

Sextant: "Consumption"

Spinning Jenny: "Catalogue for ladies in disguise"

Madison Review: "What it is like to be an outlaw," "Last pose"
Third Coast: "Starting with that time," "Look"

Research supported by the National Endowment for the Arts, Creative Artist Grant, 1999; and the Arts Foundation of Michigan in conjunction with the Michigan Council for the Arts and Cultural Affairs.

I would like to thank the Fine Arts Work Center in Provincetown, the Wisconsin Institute for Creative Writing, Ralph David Samuels Trust at Dartmouth College, and the American Antiquarian Society, which also provided time, support, and resources. This book could not have been written without the help of Mark Wunderlich, Joel Brouwer, Bruce Burgett, and Nick Flynn, who took the time to read the manuscript and offer advice on its many drafts. I would also like to thank colleagues and friends Brenda Majercin, Jesse Lee Kercheval, Ron Wallace, Cleopatra Mathis, m loncar, Maria Elena Cabellero-Robb, Michael Fox, and Jessica Messer. A lifetime of thanks to Suzanne Wise for her knowledge, inspiration, and unwavering friendship.

Parts of this manuscript also won the Major Hopwood Award in Poetry from the Avery Hopwood Awards at the University of Michigan, 1990, and a Mary Roberts Rhinehart Emerging Poets Award in 2000.

For Lama Traktung Rinpoche and Lama A'dzom Rinpoche and in honor of the lineage of Do Khenyse Yesje Dorje. For my parents and family—*all my love.*

Please search hotels and keep general lookout around railroad depots, saloons, gambling resorts, etc., and inquire of yard or train masters for his having applied for employment and of railroad trainmen for his having "beat" his way on freight or passenger trains; also search pawn shops and jewelry stores for jewelry having been pledged or sold. Also inquire of ministers, class leaders, and at Young Men's Christian Association rooms for trace of him.

He is likely to be traveling as a woman.
—Pinkerton circular, circa 1895

I

Starting with that time

he shot a man in Mendota
for calling him pretty, *hey pretty, your hair's*
like spun sunshine, and then
the man fell down dead. Son of a
tin smith, he had inherited
those quick but delicate hands, and
always went for his revolver
as quick and absentmindedly as
an itch the same way he went
for those squirrel-boned
women even smaller than himself
with breasts like shallow tea-cups.

As an outlaw, he fell in love
with the wrong women—a seamstress
who sniffed glue, who sewed
her own sleeves to her arms
and flew off a bridge; a sad-faced
war nurse; a rich Northerner
who carried her father's
jawbone in her purse—
each one disappearing more
from herself, until he found
that he was mostly in love
with the shadow of a dress,
a wrist, or the outline of a mouth
pressed to the glass on the window
of the next train leaving town.

In the meantime, he killed:
any man who could ever be called
his friend. Ambushed the town
of Independence, killed 12
at Olathe, 20 at Shawnee, tied the scalps

of those he suspected most
to his horse's bridle, and rode
west. The mayor of Lawrence,
Kansas suffocated in a well beneath
his own house as the whole
town burned, the contents of every
train and wagon turned over.

In the end he came to me
because I was the timberline, way out
west, the last stand of trees.

Each night I told him about
the guns hidden in my house:
a .44 caliber in the chamber pot, a rifle
beneath the stairs, bird guns between
folded linen, revolvers hidden
in drawers, on shelves, the four boudoir
pistols plastered in walls, wrapped
in the hair of dolls.

He hid himself inside the sheen
of Smith and Wesson, the one breech
double-barreled Winchester,
my only Navy Colt. He hid because
I was the hideout, the inert
and sturdy home where he polished
his thoughts, the timber
of each trigger, the powder
in the coffee tin, the bullets
in the freezer.

In the end, I was
the safest place for him
to put his mouth.

What it is like to be an outlaw

View back over the shoulder, crick
in the neck, suspicious of even
that three-legged dog in the road
teetering like a birthing chair.
Hand always at the gun, trigger for a
ghost in window glass. So hyper-
active, you can't keep your hands
to yourself while you sit in your
corner knitting your private angel.

A girlfriend is a hide-out, a guaranteed
front row seat at the hanging, complete
with pocket tissues. A girlfriend is a
bridge, but a bridge is a prostitute, a body
in the arch of a doorway, an arced
voyage, the noplace outlaws pass through
on the way to someplace else.
You left your holster on the floor when
you walked out, or was it your belt, your
coiled pant-legs, a rattlesnake around
the question of when we will talk again.

You who would never give up
the burned house with its punched-
out eyes, who faked suicide
in the barracks, letting blood glide
in red ribbons under the latrine door—
a man born to be bad, born
to be the family pendulum, hair coiled
like bedsprings as he strangles
the favorite pet—returned to my bed
with your wrists bandaged from some other
woman's dress, your hair smelling
of steel and campfires.

Wanted: saddle king; marauder of mines;
rustler highwayman; a well-educated, consumptive
frontier bum riding under the black flag
of Quantrill, fleet horse and six-shooter
running together like molasses; a quick-
tempered, quick-triggered alcoholic killer; a swarthy
wayfarer Don Juan escaping vigilante nooses;
an honest ribbon-handler; a swindler; a three-card
monte shark; my authentic desperado.

Woke to—my green taffeta dress stolen,
bed empty. Can't mess with the man
dressed as a woman disappearing so easily
into the crowd as lawmen back around
each other like crabs, a gun in each
claw. Reappearing on my porch at dawn,
veiled visitor breezing through the parlor—
right this way, ma'am—to the back
bedroom where I bend you over the bed,
unbutton the ripped dress, unlace
the corset, dirt, blood stuck in bars
to your ribs as I pull off the whale-bone
stays, push you down to the mattress,
the skirt a quick halo around your legs.

How he is finally accused

With men, everything is exchange:
she has a slant in her eyes—two
dashes and a red look. Conscious
of the ground beneath his feet, his
weakness. She is a dress worn thin;
he is her plump wine-flask, the certainty
with which she pulls on her
stockings. She fears: wolves
in the pantry, knife at her throat.
He steals her two sheep, hog, barrel
of cider and gets thirty stripes, his
left ear sliced off. But still she cries,
he stole my bed-ticking, my fistful
of nails, my hexes, crossed
sticks on the doorstep. It has been
years since she crept into his
bed, into his pointed slumber,
riding in and out on his breath.
Lately she holds a milkweed pod
to her breast and strokes it
like a small gray bird. The clock
hands are long oars dipping
into the sleep of her eyes. When
she does wake, it is like birds
pecking her legs, pricking her
with the motion of their wings so
that she complains, her voice
like a bird's egg in her throat cracking
as she flings her head back and
says this man is choking me.

Catalogue for ladies in disguise

Figure I

A Queen of corsets and sleeping belts;
of kitcheners worn under flannel and whip-
stitched to walking dresses; of holsters and
double-breasted jackets; of pessaries—wood,
rubber, or ivory—the wing stem turning to prevent
prolapse, spring-loaded, rubber-cupped
with a plain cloth belt. All hidden under braid
and quilled silk—these skirts, this bodice, these cuffs.

Figure II

She had seen me passing on platforms
at train stations with my hat of fancy straw.

Figure III

I remember the weight of her body
drawn, tight-laced and suspended
from the wrists fashioned above
her head. We were in the rafters
of her father's hay loft, her high-heeled
boots fastened to a ring in the floor.
I gave her a wasp-waist any gentle-
man would envy, his hands a 16-inch
tape measure.

Figure IV

The full bodice. The back breadths
of surah silk, the bustle, festooned.
Marie de Medici collar and sleeves
of white lace.

The train is always narrow, late.
Skirts are tight round my figure,
my feet too large for ladies' shoes.
Pins stuck in a small space. My head
turning back over my shoulder at
the station, looking westward.

Figure V

The ring pessary; the revolver; the wing
with ivory stem; the pelvic; spring steel.
She has her hand inside herself turning,
saying you will not feel it, you will not feel—
twisting her wrist. Lady Trouble. My hands
have always been narrow and small.

Figure VI

Hold me here, bone fingers
spreading over my hips, trailing
railroad ties. These stays plucked
from the ribs of whales are
the held-in breaths of women
waiting, and I am not

waiting, soon I will be laced
by her hands that are white
leather and elastic, that are silk
coutille, webbed and crossed up
to breasts, breast plate and holster,
spit-moistened.

Gossip

He begins by troubling your
thoughts. The egg white you drop
into a glass makes the shape
of a coffin. You wander and return
to the same spot, to the same flushed
stoop of trees; hoisted from the ground
and thrown against a stone wall;
the cart-horse's tack all flung to
pieces; and you can't lift a half
bushel of corn when he visits
disguised as a neighbor pretending
to buy a hogshead, giving you sleeves
to dye. He knocks your shovelboard
into the fire, causing your infant
to cry, your children to fall down and
bruise their faces, cuts pieces out
of your windpipe with his fingernails.
When he leaves, you see a black pig
in the hallway vanishing, returning
by the fire, vanishing. Someone left a cake
made of urine, rye in the fire-ash,
and the pig ate it. Strange arrangement
of dried peas, nails upon the fire grate.
You confess this neighbor keeps
a red rat under his shirt, poppets
made of rags and hog bristles, headless
pins. At night a light burns in
your bedroom; he comes in dressed
as a woman—red paragon bodice,
snake over his shoulder, yellow bird
in his breast; he presses his palms—two
turtles, marsh grass—to your ears
as he lays his long body

upon yours so you cannot
move as your wife snores, you are
sure you will die like this in
a lamentable manner, his tongue
a shard of ice between your teeth
as you hear him speaking: *what
is the timberline whispering
to you? Now you must listen
carefully to me.*

Rumor

that he was killed last night by _____ of Ray County. The
Deadly Weapon used. What the Slayers say. The Weeping Wife.
The question on every tongue. There is no mistake about it this
time. He was brutally murdered by two of his Pals. Shot down in
his own house. Killed with a pistol he presented to a Supposed
Friend. Wife of Outlaw to exhibit her husband's rifles, gun belts,
and pistols. The coffee mill the son was playing with when his
father was shot sells for two dollars. Notorious Outlaw wrote
letters to this newspaper under false names. Outlaw's Horse
featured in stage show at Tootle's Opera House. Member of the
Outlaw Gang dies of heart trouble. Outlaw's bones at rest in
new grave. Aged mother OK-ed move. Bullet hole and gold teeth
establish Identity. Aged mother dies on train in Oklahoma. Son
of famous Bandit Leader is now a member of the Legal
Profession. Hands Up! says Death to Bandit's Brother. Outlaw's
Blacksmith dies. Outlaw's Widow dies without telling secrets. A
Letter left to the Public: *Goodbye. All relatives stay away from me.
Reporters, be my friends. Burn me up.*

Love letter

I have buried nineteen casks of peach brandy in the back field.
Drowsiness grows on me, and I sleep with my hand brushing
    the floor,

A trap-line dropped from the bed. Mid-voyage, your lungs bled.
They could have nailed your body into one of those brandy
    barrels.

The rows of skulls in the charnel house all have your name
Gouged in their foreheads. Here at the water's edge,

I chum out my pieces, and use sweet words to lure the body:
Ribs uplift from the ocean beds, but the crabs and fish that quilt
    your face

Have picked the sockets clean. You once fed me wine from your
    mouth,
Ate only with your hands and unraveled the seams of your good
    shirts

Giving me string to sew. And before you left, you showed me
The ocean, dipping my braids in the waves and sucking them.

Because the tips were paint brushes, because they tasted
Of salt. With them, you drew trees on my stomach

Wetting and rewetting the ends with your lips.   25
"I want them to find us like this," you said, "my hands

Stitching your ribs." One day, I said, your belly
Will be snarled with my hair; it will be the net

That keeps your insides together when you are an old man.

Consumption

In the distance, guns explode again
into nothing. Everyone wears
a mourning ring on their thumb for somebody,
everyone burns belongings: sheets, petticoats, stockings.

Yet he remains haunting:
   one thousand gloves at his grave,
   ten gallons of wine for the wake,
   charcoal-belly moldering each syllabled mistake.

They say his body
must be disrupted—femur bones
crossed, a decimated chest
stitched in cere cloth, alum,
       the collapsed grave sack.
Even memory cannot save us this: decaying,
the brain slips into mouthfuls of plasma,
and fingernails tick on
     nervous in their ash-bucket skin.
He is a coffin growing hair by the second,
       and grief—
is wind in the body: no way in,
no way out, a house with no doorway,
a house of wind.

Each night he wades deeper into my chest,
lowering himself, a knee into each lung—
the way infection always starts
with lovers—my chest,
since the first time I saw him,
     a ragged, looted house.

It was trigger-happy

It was need. Misunderstanding. Joy. The idea of freedom. An old
gut wound. Festering. It was climbing out there at midnight over
the rocks just to look at the canyon of want. It was dreaming of
oceans, never having seen oceans. It was your teeth on my
thigh, my hands on your back, your arms through the iron
headboard like prison bars, my legs on your shoulders. A man
next door yelling at his dog. It was smoke, late night eating with
our hands. It was your silver rings along the bureau like bullet
shells because you are going to come over here, make love to
me, please, again. It was outlands, no trespassing, possession
without address, want, cheating, double-crossing horse-thievery,
here why not take all my chips, you still owe me money, asshole,
out past the barbed wire. The roads with no road signs, out in a
place where people can slap each other, smash cooked eggs, a
skillet against the kitchen wall of a shack in the desert where the
cactus throw their limbs in the air like dance hall melodrama,
and I have escaped to tell you all of this.

Last pose

What you see:
the outlaw, dead,
strapped to a chair.

Behind her head: a bullet hole
blooms geranium.

Above her right breast:
a secret wound
that gasps beneath
her shirt, a fish gill
underwater.

After the wounding
she lay all night in the stream,
water rushing over her chest,
a mouth that would not close.

As for her clothes, you can see
she wears a shirt striped
like bed-ticking with small rips
in the sleeves. Buttons, either
wood or ivory, felt trousers.

As a child, a homemade bomb blew
her mother's arm off
and she had to pick up
the pieces of her brother's stomach
with her hands.

If you look closely, you can
see that her hands are thin
and lady-like, with delicate

card-playing fingers and nails
of hardened corn.

Now pictured with her
arms crossed over her chest, left
hand upon right—a restful
pose. But I know only hands,
locusts rising from fields,
sewing machine needles.

Nobody knows what size
her boots were, or who stole them.
But you can see her feet
cockeyed and pale,
the roots of a yanked-out tree.

She wasn't even dead when
her mother, sleeve pinned
to her arm, sold all the pebbles
off the edge of her grave.

Finally she rode all night
for sixteen grains of morphine.
I listened to her raving,
to her sweat-thrown words,
to the mouth that opened
and closed. I walked her
in circles in my kitchen
sticking her arms with pins.

Betrayals forced her
to shoe her horses backwards
and to walk backwards

into the desert, grinning, her face
toward me, never turning
her face from mine until
she was just a wave
of heat on the horizon—
a steamship of bone,
an engine of skin. And I stood
with the hatchet between
my teeth looking
after her, no longer
meaning what I said.

Reasons why he may not have returned

That yellow bird outside your window carries the dead man's song
in its throat.

I have been known to be in two places at once, yet how am I here
in a Spanish prison all my quills broken?

What the desperate man wrote: *marry another.*
What the desperate man wrote: *wait for me.*

(When his mother died, the river flooded its banks. For weeks
he waded through the house in ankle-deep water. Her stray clothes
floated, the reflection of clouds in the parlor.)

From the beginning I could tell
that you were a woman who would braid my beard
to the bed-post, stick her hair pins in butter, salt the sheets thinking
I was a house wren, a simple bird to catch.

Even fish leave their shadows on water.
The shad-roe on the river bottom is candied jelly, your eyes
always on me.

Perhaps it is better this way: I could never love you enough.

Betrayed by the officer of the watch, I had no other choice—
arms were put in my hands. Afterwards I broke up the ship,
crafting a neat hut out of the wooden hull, and remained here
on this island.

Here on this island, women weave cloth
from the bark of trees, men wear bracelets of boar tusk, and the rain

31

comes in sideways. Everything I write turns to mud and runs
off my hands in rivers.

My enemies have gouged my eyes out, and I cannot see my way home.
Each day I drink a spirit made from my own spit.

You wouldn't want your children raised by a rogue.
I am doing you a favor. I have always considered you a lady.

(After the feast, the wedding cabbage, the large, half-eaten mutton
still on his plate, his father set out to disrupt: mourning china, the braids
of his dead mother, the bed-sheet with its red bloom, all
Indian pipes in the forest turned black by his touch.)

Perhaps it is better this way: I have loved you
far too much.

In my dreams you live in houses that burn light from the inside,
and servants throw lobsters back into the sea. In dreams I pace
rooms searching for traces of you: the scrape of your shoe across
the threshold. My coat on its peg since the night I left—my back turned
against myself.

Here, I burn seeds and nuts for light. Survive on yams, plantains, a fruit
that can become bread, and want only for axes, sharp edges for cutting.
I have had many wives, and they trust me. Each night a different one com
and lays her head in my hands.

I have thirty-five children.

Hotel suicide

Dear Nobody,

       We are the hands you left—
three fingers wire-bound and strapped
to a board, photographed. We mute
what the mind could not forget: names,
what he once said—*can never be*
taken back.

We held the braided arm, poured
carbolic acid, braced the embroidered arm, a shredding
hotel chair, watched the ceiling arms
                   stare back like cracked lilies.
We once held a key made of hair, of needle turned twice
in the velour light of a hallway sprouting rooms,
                            once knew
door lacquer, the places skin digs in,
         how to rip a suitcase full of paper.

What you gave us:
              tight grip of pen,
              your mouth, a perch on the dip
              of throat.
What you wrote: unspeakable. The collection of used things,
other people's wedding rings, bird-women
with the claws of beasts—*to be arms chained*
to the headboard, to be arms above the earth,
to have a decent burial, leaving
                 the prescriptive purse of money.
We are the hands you read: Headline pairing
Life, the mount of Moon, Venus girdle, the second
phalanx of Saturn's finger long with insanity,
the necessary condition for the act, according

33

to chirognomy journals.
                    In the morgue ten days—
transpierced, evaporated woman, not a trace, not a tooth
punctuating strewn carpets—newspapers printed
our palms instead: striated shells, bleached wood,
tiny whorls drawn up and down the shrinking tips, each
a hooded head in the flash, shadow, flash—as if
a mother or lover could claim imprinted, indelible flesh,
the routes you burned, shipwrecked—
                              all the evidence we knew.

II

I am the real Jesse James

It took four men with big heavy hands to hold the horse down. The horse kicked its stomach, collapsed like an ironing board and rolled over, pinning the legs of the men beneath it. One man sat on its neck, while the other administered the needle—Bute and Demerol in the night paddock. The horse's eyes were like stop lights in the headlights of the men's trucks parked in a circle around the animal. I have faced this animal in a paddock when it was too late to run. I was young but I was no girl when my hand came down hard on the muzzle of the horse that charged, half a ton of meat and muscle thrown my way.

*

I am the real Jesse James. I have stared down that stampede, that rage he thinks belongs only to him. I heard it took four men to hold him down when his mouth frothed and he swore and spit and bit people, had to be held down against the smashed furniture. This rumor follows him like a legend, like a bad smell. An animal that can be held down by four grown men. But what kind of animal is that? A horse that kicks its own stomach. A thought that eats away at men's guts when they are already trapped, already tamed. The one last thing that she should have told him but didn't; the one time he reached for her and she turned away. I am the real Jesse James. Not the man you may have heard of held down by four men, his friends who ran after him when he drank too much as usual and was off like a horse out of the bar and down the street and into the forest of buildings, the forest of his own thoughts, all the things he should have told her.

*

Perhaps you have heard about my legend? The one that follows me like a hangover, a bad smell. It was rage that held the big animal down in the paddock, not the heavy hands of the men who pinned it there in the dirt that wasn't a paddock really, just the circle of their trucks parked and running. This happened when I was just a girl, so it is hard to remember. I watched as it took two of them to hold the neck down and administer the needle—Bute and Demerol. One man sat on the horse's neck and said: this is one sick horse, fucking bastard. The men were angry, standing in front of their trucks after chasing the horse across the field, through a forest of trees and I wasn't supposed to follow.

*

I am the real Jesse James. I know you have heard of me. That was what I was supposed to say, the last thought before I turned my head away from him and he flew into a rage. I am the real Jesse James. But I have drunk far too much tonight. And I am just a girl. Perhaps you have heard of his legend? It took four men to hold him down in the paddock after he ran out of the bar, four of his friends to hold him down because rumor has it that he smashed some furniture. I have seen this man naked and I can tell you that he is no Jesse James. I am the real thing. I mean, I am telling you the real story now. But I have drunk far too much tonight. And I am just a girl.

*

What is known about the doctor who helped the outlaw Jesse James when he was wounded, rolling in a frothy rage and held down by four men in a paddock: he brought his doctor's bag with him. Needles, Bute, Demerol. The doctor did not know he was helping an outlaw. When he entered the circle of trucks the men had parked with the engines running, the air smelled like horses let loose from barns. The outlaw Jesse James was a small girl held down by four men. She was in a rage—having smashed furniture and split a man's lip, kicked him in the stomach. Why had the men been holding her down, the doctor asked, couldn't they see she was just a girl? The air smelled like outlaws and the girl said, I am the real Jesse James, you aren't gonna tell on me, are ya, doc?

*

The doctor lived in a red house that burned light from the inside. When he walked out the red door, the air smelled like a legend. Somewhere out in a field, four men were holding a girl down by the legs, they were kneeling on her neck. Her eyes were stop lights in the air that smelled like the men's breath, like the inside of whiskey glasses. They said they were looking for a friend who ran away and they talked about him as if he were some sort of outlaw, as if he were the real Jesse James.

*

The horse, the girl said, the horse has escaped its stall, is running out in the night, has broken out of the barn. I am no girl. And I am no doctor, the doctor thought, I am a thief. I steal from medicine cabinets. The girl rides the horse to all her private robberies. Who has stolen her horse? The doctor placed a hand on the girl's neck where the boot had been. He felt a vein pulse. A red house that burned light from the inside. Isn't it always rage, the doctor thought, that makes one body hold another to the ground like some sort of legend? The men are all outlaws. They are all little girls who need to be held down and given medicine. She needed this medicine, the men told the doctor. Her mouth was a red house that burned light from the inside. I am no girl, she said, I am the real Jesse James. The men drank too much tonight and could not find their friend. The doctor placed his bag down in a circle of dirt, in the air that smelled like whiskey. I am no doctor, he said.

*

When I was a girl, my father was a doctor who lived in a house that caught fire and burned red from the inside. He was always falling asleep with a needle in his arm, burning things down. He was always running away from his four friends, those men with heavy hands who used to chase him out of bars and down the street through a forest of buildings, his own thoughts that were filled with the smell of burned houses, horses and the outlaw Jesse James. That night I watched the men driving their trucks across the fields. The trucks stopped with their headlights in a circle, the engines running. I was riding my horse through the forest until he sweated with rage, his mouth foaming, his red coat burning from the inside against my legs. I was just a girl and I was not supposed to follow the men when they drove their trucks across the field looking for my father with his doctor's bag caught in the circle of light, his eyes burning red stop lights when he said where is my girl? And the men's hands were on him.

*

But the men were not outlaws. They held themselves down with their own hands. The doctor came with his bag and gave them clean needles. The air carried the smell of horse on its back. The men talked to each other as if they were creating a legend. Each of them said, I am the outlaw, I am the real thing, the one who ran out of the bar and into the streets and give me your hands, go ahead put your hands on me and try to hold me down now that my veins burn red from the inside. I am a horse that rolls over on your legs and pins you down. And what do you think I am? Do you think I am a girl? I am no girl. Did I tell you that before I left she let four men put their hands on her? She let them hold her down to the ground.

*

There was a girl I loved who was a legend among her friends. They said that she was prone to fly into rages and sometimes just ran out of bars and into the streets. I was no doctor, but I could tell this girl needed help. Rumor had it she smashed some furniture, burned letters, and split the lip of her friend, all because a man turned himself away from her at the wrong time. I loved her, yes, but there is no point in making a legend of it. Jesse James was shot by a friend in his own home. But in his photo, they crossed his hands over his chest in a restful pose.

Look,

this is not the West, this is
the 21st century but still as desolate—
cottonwood pollen blowing through
abandoned mansions, the ball-bearing factory,
strikers with their flap-jack placards
waving at the glance of traffic.

At the discount cinema, gunfighters name
a young Cherokee guide "Look"
because of the way she stares, because
of the way they look at her. And everyone
keeps their eyes on the horizon.
Look, you've won a set of false teeth.

Look, you've won a ghost town.
When Look closes her eyes, she sleeps
like an abandoned shopping mall,
she sleeps like the crawl space under the stairs.
She wants to inhabit the veins of a leaf,
she wants to sleep in the ear of the city's great giant.

But all the gunfighters are torch singers;
they are street lights in the wilderness.
Look does not lead them over the mountain pass.
Like Annie Oakley, she aims with mirrors
and shoots backwards. Wagon trains slow
like conches moving through conch grass.

Barns and blacksmith shops bloom
beneath the hoof of the clouded moon.
Pieces of horses, news clippings are carried off
by dogs. Cannot. Couldn't. Continue.
Some stayed, like food dropped from a plane,

and survived. Some consumed each other.

Look tries to forget her husband killed
at the trail-head—how the horizon rolled
violently in his skull hitting ferns and roots
and lichen. His skin like dried pine needles,
the blank, wagon-grease eyes. Memory is a tool
dropped in the ocean.

A cowboy rubs dirt from his neck, just off
the assembly line. He looks at her skin, thinks:
darker than saddle leather. Hindsight is the best
kind of oppression. Our children will
push up the anachronistic skyline, he says,
Step closer to the fire, let me look at you.

Some women marry houses

I

My mother, blind from the swamp-gas,
the kudzu, almost married
a gas-station—had five or six
kids in a cardboard box backyard;
almost drank motor-oil in a styro-
foam cup; almost slept
with the drawer to the register open
under ghost Esso, flies licking
lip-corners, a wide-wale
corduroy grin; almost burned
our infant skin off, birthing on those
gas-rags—
                                    But this
did not happen. She married
a meat-shop owned by a prominent
butcher. He puts a neat bullet
in the temple of every yearling.
It's painless, they don't even know
how they die. Each evening she takes
buckets outside and washes
the red walls down.

II

Each day, my grandmother walked
a bridge of stretched cat-intestines
under horse-hair power lines.

Her husband found her often inside
the belly of a violin. She was all

he ever wanted in a woman: exotic as
the parlor's Oriental, the throats
of his seven caged birds. He steamed
stripped wood and clamped it
to her body. He glued seams

and clefts above the sacral
joints he kneaded each night when
they made love, so she could sing
all those pretty high notes
from inside their polished home.

III

I live alone and love
the abandoned walls, the water-
damage, the shelf-paper
tongues lolling from cabinets, mid-morning
sunlight on telephone wires, the telephone,
the leafy, leaning second-story porch.

It's easy to love the house, so quiet
in the haze of morning windows—
it's easy to love the chimney, still warm
from last night's fire, and solid
at the center, something to put my hands upon
when no one will enter me.

With this change to indoor lighting,

with this new Zoloft prescription, your eyes have become pools
of oil in the back field the century before kitchen appliances

were invented, before the sky seeped turquoise like something
withdrawn, before spy satellites stapled down the horizon.

Now the air smells like steak, after-shave and gasoline,
like my father's slow slide into adultery, a faucet dripping

in the back of my mind. The man selling coffee at the campus
kiosk is a secret outlaw. He cuts himself for decoration—

thousands of tiny mayflies at his wrists.
Unmoved by the trend of punk teenagers and their designer dogs,

he percolates the end of the century in a spoon.
He is a pie without filling, a photograph of a whipped

man, an empty sandwich. His wounds are healing
into marks of brown crayon, into curling iron burns.

In this light my skin is the color of corsets, jars of old bust cream.
When I was sixteen, my father built a disco in the basement

with speakers that flashed lights the color of grenadine, maraschino
cherries, while in my mother's kitchen, a bowl of oranges

covered itself with a green shawl. It isn't so difficult to understand
why women over the centuries mixed their own medicine.

Why not kiss me for real, as if for the first time?
Why not write me an opera? I'm sick of your guitar strings

and that tattoo of Lacan under your arm. Let's make
ourselves famous or else get drunk. If you want, you can find me

sitting on the frozen fountain in my 19th-century clothes,
with my Judy Jetson hair, with my scarification vendor,

and my Rottweiler waiting as dutiful as a pot roast, his head in my lap.

Rendered dog

I have held the man in my mouth
all day, trying to find a place
to bury him, dig him up later.
Mailboxes gape, trees fling
their arms in the air like bad actresses,
a child in a driveway unfolds
her palm like an anemone under
a wave, her face watery
above the training wheels.

Everywhere I walk, he is cat fur,
orange peel beneath my tongue: a tincture
of needles, the taste of liver salving
the gray earth. Once, in a quarry we
slathered silt beneath shirts, bodies
in the girth of plateau, morass
of limestone scapula, backs of flat rock.
We rolled our mud-flanks
across continents. A plane glazed
the dark monitor of sky, blinking red
heartbeat, *we are still alive.* I wondered
what it would be like to hold
the earth inside me, and worried
about being interred too early, lying
naked in mud, the simple sheath of seeds.

Yet technology impedes impulse, and this
is the industrial age. In the marketplace
flesh is sucked in airtight plastic, renamed
meat. Shoppers stare at my matted
hair, my swollen mouth, the crenellated
edges of lip-flap billowing with each
breath. My painted toenails clack

on asphalt. They call me
bitch with a bad mouth. But I only
translate the man who trained me: *speak,*
fetch, and *come*. Once, everything owned
itself, and roots were dug out of meaning.
Now, even the dirt can be sold.

Brochure

See all those stars in the sky?

Relics. Keyholes. Deadwood. It isn't hard to imagine

your ghost at my bedside: dried curtains and toad skin.

That feeling I get when I'm not remembering you right.

Back then, you'd dare to shoot a man in the shin.

A woman never finishes anything.

An arrow through my neck pins me

to the wagon wheel.

After wildfire,

after the firestorm, some prairie spared the flame
still grows north of the split-rail fence: Fowl Mana,
Big Blue, Little Blue, the long bone-fingers

of Panic. These reeds will last all winter—
the flat, chair-weaving type, a stem like
a catbird's throat, Queen Anne cringed in a snow bank,

the embalmed veins of rose, bright as an arch voice.
It is November, and stalks scatter the back porch
bunched like spinal cords or birth-ropes feeding

wall to wall. They'll have a life in a gallery
assemblage, or wreathed in this dead season
of gifts. They are a hall of nothing, but not

dead, cannot be called a gift (the names of flowers),
weeds, or twigs, cannot please the sick and dying, or
be carried in on breakfast trays with squeezed juice.

Outside, a confused line of crows lifts off
the charred blanket, Open Lands. I have walked
out here, plucked the coarsest ones by hand, red and

black as your beard. Patient, tweezed after love, they talk
of root, shaft, the ragged edges left when withdrawn.
So this is Death, I thought, so this is Emptiness—

although we have had little burn damage this year,
acted early, found the boy with his hands clasped
deep in the blonde grass, match-flame rising like a hurricane.

After wildfire, the storm, Hiroshima,
black bodies stacked hospital hallways, and fell naked
in the streets like the limbs of trees, clothes singed
off backs by one moment's brilliance: Atomic-Sun.
One mother found her daughter's face
covered by a stranger's kerchief, and was grateful

for a screen to project memories upon: green
landscapes, young children, the swing-beam of light
catching dust motes, the reason why

I walk into desperation sometimes,
into the field's ground-zero—for stone,
or twig, or kerchief rising like a flag over

memory—to remember you, a face
that I now recognize, walking out
of the burned landscape—she is not a man,

she is a woman, young, barely fourteen;
she has stared at the exploding sky too long,
and been consumed by everything.

The sky is something

From their hotel windows, men are fishing for sharks.
Beneath them, I am in love with a boy with eyes dark
from his mother's apartment on the other side of the boardwalk.

I hold his tongue in my teeth in the back of a rusted truck—
80 mph over a beach dotted with bonfires.
Some part of his body is always moving—leg-twitch, fingers, arms
—like fire, like a shark sleeping.

At fifteen, photographs of water make me seasick with longing.
I wear the same T-shirt for weeks,
                                        charming myself. WBCN, "The Rock
of Boston," and the sun setting over my body that is hookey
from dance studios, from moving in unison,
in leotards and jazz shoes, from moving
up the back staircase to my own coiled room.

The boy's hair smells like cumin, tumeric,
like his mother's doughy arms, like soup cooking.

Tell me something beautiful, I say to him; what two bodies can do.
Beautiful—like the speed of the truck, cheap beer,
the forced squint of his face against wind, beer, sun—*the sky,* he says,
the sky is something.

I think of the fishermen: the smell of shark on their finger tips,
the stained hotel pillows.
Love is an arm roped in fishing line: invisible,
cutting. I suck the small gold cross on the chain
at my neck like a restaurant mint, wonder
what it will be like to finally lie next to him: the still compartments
of his eyes, his skin of rough stones, and his incessant motion,
even when sleeping, as if his heart, swimming into his throat,
wanted to be caught there.

In the market,

a transaction is made, and the snake
is lifted from the basket by the back
of its head, the body dangling
like a girl's braid. With a flash
of silver the head is scissored
into Tupperware and the skin
peeled down like a condom, like the arm
of a wet shirt, the slick inner
muscle exposed and thrown
to the counter like a party ribbon.

Now the animal is pure meat,
the long cords pulled apart
from the spine, a broken zipper.
The customer wants only
the liver, the size of a lover's earlobe,
said to improve brain function,
to replace lost memory.

Memory can become a medicine that,
clamped beneath the tongue, heals
all past and recent conflagrations.
But scars are the prisons skin builds
around injury, the angle of the roof
increasing as each blade is drawn in
and out. And memory is the room
where you wait in the dark.

You still had your key. You heard
my footstep on the landing, the tumblers
rolling in the lock. You sat like a priest
at the edge of the sofa, your clothes
the color of earth and organs, like an animal

caught at the roadside, you wanted
to catch me with a new lover,
my nylons already shed, limp in my
hand, returning at 3 a.m.

Above the market's temporary roofs,
the tin and blue plastic, it is raining.
Below them, the butcher has killed
five snakes. He works on the sixth,
his fingers plying the spinal cord,
his face jiggling. The customer stares
at the organs pinning down the paper
towel—gray ghost bodies, five tiny fists.

He looks like you: like there is
something lost to him, something
he doesn't even realize yet
that he has forgotten to say, something
that was stripped away by a larger
man's hands moving down a tiny spine,
in childhood, in the dark, his fingers
hooked into the softest places, into
the coiled knot of thighs and clamped
jaws snaking away beneath footsteps
in the hall, beneath the rotting house sill,
the roots and leaves and soiled market
basket, the locked back rooms.

The customer is asking for two
more, wanting to know how
this will work, this new world
where nothing is forgotten even this
feeling that sometimes makes him strike

at nothing, that makes him glide
as if dreaming, side-winding
in the night, his body triggered, one long
hearing instrument spread out upon
the earth, the path up from the garden—
and his hand stays perched
at the collar bone like yours was when
the shard of light, my shadow,
entered the house—your hand pale
against your shirt like a poised wing,
like the snake arched, waiting.

Dear America,

You who love the teenage boy,
who comes to you with milk
pouring from his skin, who when
he enters you makes smoke, snakes, creeping
vines pour from your skin.
You are in the guest room, America,
and the mother has taken the sister
to tennis lessons, and the universe
is about to begin, upstairs, off
center, in the spare room where
holiday decorations are stacked
in boxes—tinsel and stars, cans
of hairspray, high school honor roll
plaques, cub scout medals and the faded
hats of the dead grandmother
who was the last person who slept
in this room, her spine curved
like a question mark on top
of the pilled bedspread.

What happens next?
The skin below the boy's neck
tastes like underwater plants, wet
wool and cotton, like syllables
inside your mouth before they form,
emotions that can teach the tongue.

Later in support groups you will say
he didn't know what a clitoris was.
You will say that it was in a basement,
not a bedroom, and that he sort of
made you. Because no one wants to
imagine that right now you are leading

the boy by the hand upstairs past framed
family portraits, that you are pushing
the parkas, the boxes of canceled checks
off the bed. No one, because
you are just a girl.

Downstairs, ants slowly unpack
the drains, flies spin on their backs
in window sills like uneaten
vitamins and the kitchen holds
its mouth closed in the place where you
sat from 3:10 to half past four
at the table, hands clasped
around glasses of Quick that sweated
with barometric pressure, and those
precarious, empty upstairs rooms.

Above you, his bedroom walls
flap with posters of tight-crotched
rock stars, his sister's doll lamps
blink under lace canopies, and his parents'
waterbed holds the exact temperature
inside the body, as you hold him
inside your body, America, everyone thought
you were a girl, but really you are
this teenage boy who has been singing
Top 40 all summer—tunes about drowned girls
and convoys and rivers and dead
towns and outlaws stretching
their arms out to the silver
highways—and you have unbuckled
the belt, shed the jeans, the plaid
boxers, you are lying back

on the bedspread, your arms outstretched,
you are looking at yourself in the face
of freedom, in the spacious skies of
the mirror that rises out of your body,
(what the body of another might feel like)
the body of the lover above your body
lying in the mirror above the bed—
                                    and you look up
to her now like a magazine, a billboard,
the horizon you might have had.

Song

This house is a cyclone,
but I have a trap door
inside my throat.

Even now that the bed has given up
its belief in the body,
we can still lie down
together in our brokeness.

The problem is the wind tunnel.
The problem is I want
what you breathe.

And I've caught history
like an illness. Someone has
opened the flue, and we've all
gone to the basement
for tornado warnings. The roof
flies off like a board game,
and all the windows are
punched-out dominos.

The problem is you do not
exist, and I have too many
lovers now. One says stay
in the doorway; one says
this ladder has hooves;
one has her mouth pressed
against the door between
her legs; one says Coast Guard
calling on the other extension, it's
for you.

You are the song on hold,
and we are all in the basement
curled around the furnace,
its body a dark animal panting.
The wind outside roars.
My eyes grow in the dark.

It is you I want to hold
in my mouth—this emptiness,
ash from the furnace, our
burnt and drowned things,
this dust and bone chip, this
moment, taste of paper, finger
grease, and how you always
used to breathe in my mouth
the moment when I'd say let me
hear you sing, now that
your chest explodes with its own joy.

Notes

"How he is finally accused," and "Gossip" were inspired by the transcript of the trial of Bridget Bishop, who was accused and convicted of witchcraft, Salem, Massachusetts, 1692.

"Catalogue for ladies in disguise" is a compilation of text from an 1891 corset catalogue. Pessaries were used to prevent the collapse of the uterus and other organs caused by the tight-lacing of corsets. They were made of wood, rubber, ivory, or steel, and were removed at night or during sexual intercourse.

"Rumor" mimics headlines and newspaper articles about Jesse James and his family.

"Reasons why he may not have returned" was inspired in part by the ship's log of Captain Mayhew Folger c. 1809, Clemens Library at the University of Michigan, Ann Arbor, MI. In 1808, Folger's ship, the Topaz, landed at Picarin Island in the South Pacific and met the man known as "Alec," or Alexander Smith, the last surviving mutineer of the famous mutiny of the Bounty. All other mutineers had been killed in a slave uprising. The slaves were then murdered the next night by the dead men's widows, Alec being the only adult male survivor.

"Hotel suicide" refers to an incident in 1898, when an unidentified woman checked into the Chittenden Hotel and, over the course of three days, systematically destroyed all evidence of her identity. She then committed suicide by drinking carbolic acid and pouring it over her face. She left only a brief note and a purse full of money asking for a decent burial. Her identity was never discovered, yet a photograph of her hands was supposedly published in local newspapers. I came across the photograph of her hands in a 1940's palmistry journal which described the lines in her palms as exhibiting "the necessary condition for the act."

"Brochure" includes found text from rest area brochures advertising Wild West tourist sites off I-80 in the states of Wyoming, Colorado, and California.

"Some Women Marry Houses" is the first line of Anne Sexton's poem, "Housewife."

photo by Todd Berliner

Sarah Messer has received fellowships from the Fine Arts
Work Center in Provincetown, the Wisconsin Institute for
Creative Writing, the American Antiquarian Society, and the
National Endowment for the Arts. She is a graduate of the
Masters of Fine Arts program at the University of Michigan.
A memoir of place, *Red House*, is forthcoming from Viking.
She teaches poetry and creative nonfiction at the
University of North Carolina-Wilmington.

New Issues Poetry & Prose

Editor, Herbert Scott

James Armstrong, *Monument in a Summer Hat*
Michael Burkard, *Pennsylvania Collection Agency*
Anthony Butts, *Fifth Season*
Gladys Cardiff, *A Bare Unpainted Table*
Joseph Featherstone, *Brace's Cove*
Lisa Fishman, *The Deep Heart's Core Is a Suitcase*
Robert Grunst, *The Smallest Bird in North America*
Mark Halperin, *Time as Distance*
Myronn Hardy, *Approaching the Center*
Edward Haworth Hoeppner, *Rain Through High Windows*
Janet Kauffman, *Rot* (fiction)
Josie Kearns, *New Numbers*
Maurice Kilwein Guevara, *Autobiography of So-and-so: Poems in Prose*
Ruth Ellen Kocher, *When the Moon Knows You're Wandering*
Steve Langan, *Freezing*
Lance Larsen, *Erasable Walls*
David Dodd Lee, *Downsides of Fish Culture*
Deanne Lundin, *The Ginseng Hunter's Notebook*
Joy Manesiotis, *They Sing to Her Bones*
David Marlatt, *A Hog Slaughtering Woman*
Paula McLain, *Less of Her*
Sarah Messer, *Bandit Letters*
Malena Mörling, *Ocean Avenue*
Julie Moulds, *The Woman with a Cubed Head*
Marsha de la O, *Black Hope*
C. Mikal Oness, *Water Becomes Bone*
Elizabeth Powell, *The Republic of Self*
Margaret Rabb, *Granite Dives*
Rebecca Reynolds, *Daughter of the Hangnail*
Martha Rhodes, *Perfect Disappearance*
Beth Roberts, *Brief Moral History in Blue*

John Rybicki, *Traveling at High Speeds*
Mary Ann Samyn, *Inside the Yellow Dress*
Mark Scott, *Tactile Values*
Diane Seuss-Brakeman, *It Blows You Hollow*
Marc Sheehan, *Greatest Hits*
Sarah Jane Smith, *No Thanks- and other stories* (fiction)
Phillip Sterling, *Mutual Shores*
Angela Sorby, *Distance Learning*
Russell Thorburn, *Approximate Desire*
Robert VanderMolen, *Breath*
Martin Walls, *Small Human Detail in Care of National Trust*
Patricia Jabbeh Wesley, *Before the Palm Could Bloom:*
    Poems of Africa